I was.
I am.
I will be.

Blay G.

Copyright © 2019 Blay Gnahore

All rights reserved.

ISBN: 9781092161671

DEDICATION

I dedicate this book to my family, who over the years, have kept my head above water when I've felt that I'm drowning. I dedicate this to my friends who have been there to share the weight on my shoulders when I've felt like I can't walk any further. I dedicate this to my girlfriend who has the ability to make me feel like the most special being to live. Finally, I dedicate this to everyone who has supported my poetry that I've been releasing over the years. Thank you. This is my first book. Written and edited by myself. It can only get better from here.

CONTENTS

You should know.

1	I Found	Pg 8
2	I Hurt	Pg 28
3	I Fell	Pg 62
4	I Rose	Pg 82

YOU SHOULD KNOW

I was structured when I decided that I was going to write this book. I had a girlfriend that would motivate me to be the best person I could possibly be, I also had the motivation and ambition that success was right around the corner. That all came to an end so suddenly.

I lost her, I lost my ambition, I lost my heart & overall I stopped caring about what happens next. This book was meant to be motivation in the form of poetry. The message was supposed to be that all that starts badly will end well. However now, I don't know where it ends or how it ends so I guess all I can say is only time will tell.

Have you ever felt like you gave your all
to people who wouldn't even take notice
if you took a bullet for them?
Have you ever felt like you've been taken for granted
by people you constantly tried to show how much
they mean to you?
Have you ever been constantly rejected by the same
person that you show nothing but love towards?
If you've ever felt any type of pain from love
then what you're about to read will trigger
some unwanted feelings. Don't stop reading.

1

I was. I am. I will be.

You were the introduction to this emotion that was
so rare to me,
The genesis of my love story, the big bang that
created a new universe for you and me,
Where we were the only two who knew how it felt to
be this deep in infatuation,
Obsessed with your whole being, I knew how far
we'd go from our very first conversation.
Do you remember it? I do so clearly,
The first time we connected, I couldn't stand not
having you near me.
They say that absence makes the heart grow fonder,
Well I'm sorry that your absence made my effort
slumber,
If it wasn't for you I'd never know what it felt like to
be this deep in love,
I kept our memories intact even though it's been a
year since we've broken up,
I have hope that one day we'll be able to continue
what we once had,
When I lost you I lost it all, so even though I have
money now, in my eyes there isn't much more that I
have.
It used to warm my heart when we'd chill out and
talk about what the future holds,
Now I chill on my own, thinking about what I've lost
and how it's turned me cold.
This is a book of my emotions, through poetry, it
shall be told.

Take my hand on this journey as I welcome you to
my soul.

Blay .G.

Her beauty delves deeper than what the eye can capture.
Her past clings on to her present like a child that doesn't want to leave his mother on the first day of school.
All she has experienced is betrayal so anytime she's shown attention, she questions who else is receiving it.
Anytime she's shown love, she questions how they plan to benefit from it.
It was written in the scriptures that your body is a temple and my only intentions are to worship.
I understand that trust is such a hard thing to give nowadays considering that the ones that appear to be the most sincere could be the same ones whispering sweet lies of hope into your ear.
Let me be the drug that numbs your pain. I've always found beauty in imperfection and so in showing me your flaws, you caught my attention.
An outcome that you may not have intended.
As I write this, I picture your face lying next to mine, I picture you as I wake up and get the same feeling I had when I graduated and received a round of applause.
I can only assume it's because you are one of my greatest rewards.

I was. I am. I will be.

Do you believe in Soulmates? Let me explain to you how beautiful mine is.
She's the type of girl that can look at you and draw your soul right through your iris,
I never understood why I exist but you gave me purpose and reason for why I live,
I look at you now and see my whole future ahead of me,
It's like you're a slideshow of everything that's meant to be,
A TV screen full of joys and screams from our little seeds,
Switch the scene,
Now it's you and I living together.
You don't ever have to leave, not now not ever.
It's the dream,
But for now we're still young, so I'll wait for those days to come,
Nevertheless, when it's time to meet,
I'm more excited than a kid at 11:59 on Christmas eve.
Seeing your smile brings me peace, being with you puts me at ease,
After spending time with you I'm always guaranteed a good night's sleep.

Blay .G.

You are my Best friend,
Before you came into my life I knew our souls had already met,
It's as if I had married you in the spiritual and meeting you physically was the next step.
You are my soulmate,
I will protect you as long as your heart beats with mine,
A clock is a lonely man's way of living, your pulse dictates my time.
You are my muse,
My art is simply a reflection of our connection,
Your love is the GPS that guides my words in the right direction.

I was. I am. I will be.

My heart just did a bungee jump when I thought
about how long you'll be gone,
I'll think about your voice when I hear your favourite
songs,
I'll think about your laughs when I watch your
favourite shows,
I'll think about how you get so relaxed when I stroke
your back and rub your toes.
If this is meant to be then the distance will not break
us,
If God made you for me then it's not a "Goodbye
my love" but "Darling, I'll see you later".

Blay .G.

Yesterday I heard a song that reminded me of you,
The feeling that glided through my spirit was one that I was once familiar to.
I wasn't sure whether to feel content at the fact that happiness still exists in me but locked away somewhere in my spirit,
Or depressed at the fact that you're the only one that holds the key to unlock the safe that holds my heart in it.

I was. I am. I will be.

The first time I met you I saw a flower that grew through the concrete,
I saw a missing piece of my puzzle that I needed to be complete,
The tears that you cried became insecurities inside,
But as long as I'm by your side,
It's in me that you can confide,
Love can come around twice,
Don't be the fool that believes once a flower has lost all its petals that it has died,
It takes water to revive and TLC to survive,
Once you cut off what was killing it, it'll blossom back with life.
You're that flower in my eyes, without the ring you're still my wife,
We're so different but so alike and with that smile, you can make all the 8 planets align,
With that smile, you can pause time and make my heart stop but ironically that same smile makes me feel so alive.

Blay .G.

I often hear the expression 'it was written in the stars' but only God himself could have written a story like ours. We both came from backgrounds that made us lose hope in the L word, but that hope was returned when our universes merged.
I use these words to express just how deep I fell for you,
I was in heaven when we were together but the floor broke and I fell right through.
I no longer have the privilege of experiencing your presence.
It was as appreciated as a present gifted from the higher-ups to the peasants.
If we could make this work again I'll give you all I have to offer because I know what we shared will not be able to be recreated with any other.
If you're in pain then I'll suffer because I feel what you feel,
I'll be your doctor, your medication and anything you need to heal,
I kept it real from the start, I showed you the scars on my heart,
Because I knew deep down it's you I wanted to be facing when the priest made me promise 'till death do us apart'.

I was. I am. I will be.

You always told me that you wish your eyebrows
were more full,
But they emphasise the true beauty of your eye
colour.
You say you wish your stomach was slimmer,
But I love it,
It's a comfort for me when I lay my head upon it.
You wish your boobs were a bigger size,
But they're my exact cup of tea.
You wish your skin was another complexion,
But our skins rejoice when connected like two love
birds on a tree,
You say you have so many flaws,
But they're all attractions to me.

Blay .G.

I thought I'd been in love twice in my life. Two completely different experiences. One drained my energy whereas the other replenished it. One made me see myself as a king whereas the other made me view myself as a pawn. One made me feel secure whereas the other kept me questioning.
The second time I fell, I made myself believe that they were the same but they were not the same at all, The only similarity was that they were both conditional.

I was. I am. I will be.

I admire from a distance,
Her beauty is overwhelming like the scent of my mother's food on Christmas,
You are the dream that I pray comes to reality,
You are my wishes that I hope one day come true,
From asking what's your name to will you marry me,
I pray I can spend my life with you,
We're all living to die, I'm just searching for a person that I can share this journey with,
Someone I can see eye to eye and feel confident that this bond will be strong for as long as I live.

Blay .G.

It's not about how deep you fall but rather if they have the strength to catch you,
After all, if you fall into strong arms then you will feel no harm,
but fall into arms that are not and you're bound to feel the impact of the drop,
Your whole world will feel scattered, as your heart starts to shatter,
But if they're secure then the height from which you fall won't even matter.

I was. I am. I will be.

I blessed my face with your holy juices while I spoke
to your sacred pink pearl in tongues,
I baptised my nose in your pool until you caught the
holy ghost and felt no air pass through your lungs.

I think I made you cum.

Blay .G.

The love that I crave is not one of the new age,
It has nothing to do with social media likes or reassurance from strangers.
I prefer that old school love,
That talk to each other on the phone till we both doze off,
And even then, the conversation has still not come to an end,
Because when we wake up, we pick up where we left off and the whole process starts again.
I want that best friend love,
You can tell me about anything and anyone that's winding you up,
I could sit there and listen to you talk about what your fake friends have been doing or the juicy gossip at work that's going on,
I want you for life and if that means running the longest marathon,
Then for you,
I'll put on my running shoes and make sure I go above and beyond.

I was. I am. I will be.

My sweet pretty pink.
The more I rub you, the more you cry.
Why?
I kissed your lips and you let out a sigh,
When I was hungry you fed me,
When I needed a place to unload,
You invited me to cum inside.
I know that if things ever get hard,
You'll handle them and ride.
It's like we're a perfect fit,
I love that sweet pretty pink of mine.

Blay .G.

I call you Medusa,
Because anytime you stare directly in my eyes I turn harder than stone,
What we have is rare,
I see the snakes trying to get into your head but ignore them because when we connect we bond stronger than sodium and chlorine,
I'll make your body feel like it's in heaven,
Let me be your shot of morphine.

I was. I am. I will be.

You say my smooth words have you falling head
over heels,
I'll put your heels beside your head to have a late-
night meal,
You said I touch you in your weak spots,
I guess I've found your Achilles heel,
I'll have you on my sofa, giving me a piece of your
mind like we're on Dr. Phil,
There are only 8" inches that come between us,
You're already moaning and I've only given you half
of all I have like we've agreed on a prenup,
I'm sure you've been told to never let food go to
waste,
So eat this meal below my waist
And when you're done,
Shall I put my icing on your cake?

Blay .G.

You need to comprehend that it's you that I plan to share my life with, the universe brought us together to create an emotional hybrid,
A feeling that God has provided, within my heart he has ignited, when we're united I feel excitement but Sadness when we're divided,
I see the beauty in your eyes but deeper down I see a heart that cries,
I see a soul that's been crushed by false hopes, sold dreams and lies,
I see a mind that's been filled with memories of pain that has been disguised,
but what you don't know is that I thank God for your existence every night,
I thank God for ridding me of the darkness by using your light.
The laws of gravity have been defied because even with everything holding me down you still managed to help me rise.

I was. I am. I will be.

Your body is an instrument and I am the musician,
I feel your vibrations every time I strum
which lead to a sensual sound whether it be with my
fingers or with my tongue.

You are my little guitar.

Blay .G.

2

I was. I am. I will be.

You need to understand that not everybody that
comes into your life is here to stay,
But they all leave a memory,
One which will either remain,
As a beautiful painting or an irremovable stain.

Blay .G.

If you've found love, cherish it because this may be
your only chance to have it,
The lucky ones find it twice and the unlucky don't
get that advantage,
The smart ones see what they have so they refuse to
stray no matter how hard it may get,
The dumb ones do then start to regret when they see
their source of happiness...

..vanish.

I was. I am. I will be.

The stars used to seem so far away until I lost the
love of my life.
I found out that distance can be changed with the
state of your mind,
I felt so close to you no matter where you were when
you were mine,
But then we'd argue and I'd feel a mile away while
laying right by your side.

Blay .G.

You came into my life once already when I wasn't
searching,
Made me see myself as a blessing rather than
somebody's burden,
Is it too farfetched to think that somewhere in the
distant future,
You and I can make it work again?
Hopefully as a better version
than what we once were.

I was. I am. I will be.

Would it be too late if I asked if we could try again?
I know that you said we may be better off as friends
but there's no way that I can stand here and pretend like
I'm okay with this to end.
Only you know how deep I fell,
So my mouth will always wish you well,
But my heart... My heart...
still wishes you were with me.

Blay .G.

I questioned if I'd ever hear from her again,
Regret filled my head every time I thought about my actions,
That one night of dishonesty has caused my entire future to be fractured,
How did I lose the heart of a rare one after it took ages to be captured?
'Boys will be boys' is the excuse that our mums used when we were growing up,
But they never warned us that the excuse cannot be used on love,
They never warned us that heartbreak can make us feel so numb,
They never warned us that even though women are emotional beings, certain situations can make men just as soft.

I was. I am. I will be.

When I first met you, I had dreams of a wedding.
You're wearing your white dress and I'm wearing my
grey suit,
But the one thing I never knew,
Is that the guests would be dressed in grey,
And it would be black for the groom.
Congratulations.

Blay .G.

Do you know how it feels to lose somebody that
became such a significant part of your life,
So meaningful that they also became part of you, so
when you act you think of them in everything that you
do,
That means the pain that they feel, you sympathise
and feel it too,
And when they're happy and they're smiling then
your moods over the moon,
But when they go, there's a confusion because now
they're nowhere to be seen.
Our heartstrings were intertwined but now you've
gone my heart's finding it hard to beat,
You were the main source of my happiness and now
I'm finding it hard to be,
Anything that I was when I was with you because
you're no longer a part of me.

I was. I am. I will be.

Some people are Gold,
Others are Gold plated,
Learn to distinguish between the two because they
may both glow in the beginning,
But only one remains the same,
The other changes and shows its true colour over
time.

Blay .G.

Loneliness is the key that opens the door to many strangers.
We tend to accept anyone to rid the feeling
While not paying attention to the fact that in exchange for your loneliness, you're potentially sacrificing more.
You're thinking about that ex that once made you happy but you're forgetting who he became.
You're thinking about that boy that was doing the most to get your attention but forgot that he ended up being the same.
You're thinking about the friends that you once cut off because they always left you mentally drained.
You're going to keep falling back into this pit of loneliness as long as you keep making the same mistakes.

I was. I am. I will be.

After the breakup, I constantly gave myself to other
girls like I had something to prove,
Every time I did it to show myself that I have moved
on from you,
But how was I meant to move on when you're the
only true love I knew?
I found myself searching for everything you are every
time I met someone new,
This is what landed me in the situation I faced last
year,
Where I was so determined to make it work with her
that I wasn't seeing clearly,
That the girl I used to replace you was nothing more
than a distraction,
From the fact that you have still had my full heart,
not just a piece nor a fraction.

Blay .G.

I really don't know whether to thank you
for showing me what I truly deserve
or whether to hate you for making me think I wasn't
enough.
I went through a hard time trying to
fathom the fact the one I was in love with left me
because it was one of my biggest fears
But from that, I learned that the people
that we often promise to give the world to
Don't necessarily see us worth being in theirs.

I was. I am. I will be.

He never showed you that he wanted you
Until you threatened that you'll leave,
He tried to change you from what you are
into what he wanted you to be.

His promises were always empty,
Because his actions never matched,
Yet you're crying over a man,
That doesn't care that you're no longer part of his long term plan.

You deserve better,
Your worth should never be traded in for love,
Because most of the time you'll just end up getting robbed,
They'll take everything you have, and give nothing back,
Respect yourself, Respect your worth,
Because this will define the type of man that you attract.

Blay .G.

You're not a traitor for leaving.
You're not weak for choosing to no longer deal with something that made you unhappy.
You're not selfish for putting your happiness first.
The purpose of a relationship is for two souls to unite in order to make each other's lives more of a desirable experience. If the relationship you're in does not give you this feeling, then you have to question the person that you're with.

I was. I am. I will be.

Once you become aware that being alone does not equate to being unwanted you will recognise your self-value. Once you grasp the concept that that being wanted is not the same as being deserved you will understand that not just anyone should be allowed to have you.

Blay .G.

What cuts deep is not the fact that you left.
It's knowing that I could have changed my ways to prevent it,
I was the cause of your departure, give me a moment to vent this,
I took a good girl for granted, I used your kindness to my advantage,
You were my future and when you left I saw no way of advancing,
We went from Dm's, BBM to calls through the PM,
I heard you got a new man now, you got me wishing I can be him.
From the bottom of my heart, I wish you all the best,
Because you're a princess and you don't deserve to be treated like anything less,
I want to see a smile on your face even if it's not me that put it there,
It's crazy because I never pictured us in this position right here,
I dreamed of us living together, watching movies while I play with your hair, now reality feels unfair,
So I go to sleep at night just to escape this nightmare.

I was. I am. I will be.

People's emotions should not be a tool you use to
get over your last,
So stop making people believe there's a future for
them with you,
When in fact, for you, they're just an escape from
your past.

Blay .G.

Have you ever heard of a wolf in sheep's clothing?
Many girls make the mistake of giving themselves to a man when they barely know him.
You are so quick to give your heart and your time to people and then regret it later,
Because the last one broke your heart so you think this one will save you,
But like a deception, they mask their true self with a false persona,
But vultures prey on the weak, disguise themselves into the one you seek,
So ask God to open your eyes and you may be surprised at what you see.

I was. I am. I will be.

I am convinced that you were a surgeon in your past life
the way you were able to tear me apart and remove my
heart without leaving a scar or maybe you were a
mechanic,
Because piece by piece you took me apart,
Like a car, but still, that wasn't enough.
You were the hypnotist that made me believe that this
was really love.

Blay .G.

I chose you and we made all of these memories together,
And I regret it now that you're gone
But these memories are with me forever.

I was. I am. I will be.

The worst part isn't that I won't be able to
Kiss you when I see you,
Or hug you when you leave,
Or stare at you in amazement,
Knowing that it's not "I" anymore, it's "We",
It's that I have to pretend I'm okay
With seeing you doing all these things
With someone else that's not me.

Blay .G.

I was trying to express every emotion that I felt,
But not once did my pen touch the page.
I decided to call it quits, I was done writing for the day,
Then it dawned on me.
This blank page could not have described how I felt in
A better way.

I was. I am. I will be.

Often, they say 'you don't know what you got until it's gone',
But it's even worse when you know exactly what you had and have to watch it leave.

Blay .G.

Do you know how it feels to lose the person that brought the most joy into your life,
The one that you would call on if things are going bad,
The same one that will make sure that all those wrong things go right.

Do you know the regret you feel knowing that they wouldn't have left if it was up to them,
But you pushed them to a limit where they no longer had the strength to deal with or pretend,
That everything will go back to normal again.

Do you know how it feels to know you've hurt the person you love the most,
The person that you promised to take care of their heart like the most valued brick of Gold,
Yet your actions contradicted every single promise you told.

Do you know how it feels to be the cause of your own heartbreak?
Do you know how it feels?
I still can't believe that this is real.

I was. I am. I will be.

I find it hard to move on from you and it's not because
I'm obsessed,
But rather because you still partly have a hold on the left
side of my chest,
Your face is imprinted in my head and the memories
don't help,
I wish I could pretend that I'm over you and into
someone else,
But the truth is that I'm not and everything reminds me
of you,
When I'm watching a movie,
I miss being asked questions to which I respond 'I don't
have a clue',
I used to get a little annoyed but now I think of it, it was
cute,
You were my rib, my heart, the one I planned to give a
ring,
but when I lost you I lost it all and now I don't have a
thing.

Blay .G.

Loneliness is a hallucinogen,
It'll make the last resorts seem more appealing,
It'll blind your heart and thoughts as well as what you're feeling,
It'll ignore all the red flags and persuade you with reasons,
As to why being alone is worse than being in the company of a demon,
But you have to question,
Do you love him or are you just too comfortable to leave?
Because it seems that even though he brings you stress and doesn't attend to your needs,
You still can't say it with your chest that "this isn't the man for me",
You keep looking at potential not realising that that potential is not reality,
But rather a dream that we wish for reality to be.

I was. I am. I will be.

Just because their lips are touching yours, this does not
mean that it's you that they're kissing,
Your lips are only a canvas.
With their eyes closed, their mind can paint you into the
person they're missing.

Blay .G.

The same mouth that you used to tell me 'I love you'
later was used for your lies and deceit,
As you already bad karma doesn't ever come cheap,
You may think that you've gotten off for free,
But you haven't, so you will,
Have to pay the price God gives you when he hands you
your bill.

I was. I am. I will be.

You know when you're getting hurt.
You know when there's a cure for the pain.
You know that the right thing to do is leave but
You keep thinking about what you're going to lose,
Rather than what you will gain.

Blay .G.

They can't get closure so they try to weave themselves back into your life,
Then try to highlight the good times but the foundation is ruined,
Do you think a couple of sweet words will make me blush,
Then I'm going to brush it all over, what the hell are you doing?
I'm deleting pictures off my Mac because I know we aren't going to make up,
You concealed your true colours, but now it's time to show your face off.
It's finally come to the end of the masquerade,
I keep convincing myself that you act this way to mask your pain,
I would have called you family like we had the same blood running through our veins,
But now you're just somebody that I used to know, I guess I'm Gotye.

I was. I am. I will be.

I told her that I loved her and she replied show me,
don't tell me,
Because every man that she allowed herself to believe
she was loved by, came and left with a piece of her,
So now she associates love with pain,
But I'm here to make sure that her image of love is no
longer the same, I told her I'm here to bring change,
She said show me, don't tell me.
Because every man that told her that they'll bring change
to her life,
Came and destroyed any last part of her existence that
felt right,
They laid seeds of insecurity which grew into a lack of
self-confidence and voices in her head that'd tell her that
she'll never be good enough.
She no longer sees her self-worth but I told her that I
will show her just how much she means to me by using
more than words,
But her insecurities were so strong she fell for the same
trap,
She went and left me for a dream seller,
Now she's shouting, 'Men are trash'.

Blay .G.

For now, it may seem like the grass is greener
On the other side,
But it's only a matter of time
Before the seasons change
And that grass you so heavenly admired no longer looks
the same
But by then it'll be too late.
You should have stuck with me.

I was. I am. I will be.

She said she will never be able to love again,
So I made repairing her broken heart a part of my plan,
She gave it to me, I promised her that I'll take care of it
the best way that I can,
But when it was fully healed,
She went and gifted it to another man.

Blay .G.

3

I was. I am. I will be.

He constantly cried for attention hoping that one day he'll be taken notice of,
He'd do anything to get some eyes on him but he felt as if he was ignored by everyone, even God,
He began to lose sight of himself and become somebody else,
Trying to be like those that were given the attention and constant loving,
But what he failed to realise is that with every cry he made,
Formed a sea of tears that drowned his identity and his name,
As time went by the person he once was, began to fade,
Now he's got the attention he wanted but doesn't know who he is today.

Blay .G.

I question my sanity on a daily basis.
Whether life has made me lose sight of the direction I
want to go or whether my past traumas have opened my
eyes so that I can show the world through my words,
How I was blessed with a curse, to give people a better
life but result in mine becoming worse.
I dedicated my heart, soul, and mind,
I gave people most of my time so that I can listen to
their problems, but their darkness covered my shine,
Now I don't know who I can turn to or who will
live up to their favourite lie:
"I got you".

I was. I am. I will be.

Learn the difference between depression and a mood,
A mood can be cured by minor things like jokes and food,
Depression is that enemy that's constantly on your case,
So even when you manage to cheer up a little, he'll take you right back to that dark place.
That feeling of being unloved and that no one will ever relate to you,
That your life isn't worth much so you might as well end it instead of seeing it through,
So please stop telling people with depression that it's all in their head,
Because mine was the very reason I nearly ended up dead.

Blay .G.

I befriended depression and lost contact with happiness,
Depression is that friend that you'd call a pessimist,
Because she's so quick to destroy any hope of joy,
She's jealous too, anytime I even think of happiness she starts to get annoyed,
Then she reminds me of all the times that happiness came and left,
How every time I'd think she's there to stay, she disappears and leaves me a mess,
Depression always tells me that I don't need her as a friend,
and how nobody needs me so I should bring it to an end.

I was. I am. I will be.

"I'm fine", two words that can save you from a series of questioning,
A smile, one action that can blind them from seeing any hurt that you're experiencing,
A laugh, one sound that can fool the naked ear into believing all is well,
But emotion is something you can lie to everybody about except for yourself.

Blay .G.

The darkness became a part of me. I remember looking in the mirror and feeling hate,
I remember not being able to leave my bed in fear that it may be my last day,
My mind was unpredictable, I can't believe I've come this far,
As long as I breathe I made a vow to myself to never again get consumed by the dark.

I was. I am. I will be.

I already feel dead inside,
So would it even matter if at this point I take my own life?
All these thoughts in my head haven't got me thinking right,
They are telling me life is a car ride and I should just enjoy the drive but this journey has made me road sick,
Too many times I've tried to join in but it seems like there's no fit for me to be in society with the rest of you.
I'm a loner, a weirdo and I don't know what else to do but try to find a way that I can leave without bringing pain.
I picture my mother questioning where she went wrong,
I picture my sisters crying their tears listening to my songs,
I picture my brother being strong keeping up face while inside he's really crumbling,
And my dad doing the same except I will not know if he'll even feel anything,
I'm lost.
This depression really has me at a standstill,
I seem to be helping others but for my own life, I'm slowly losing the will to continue.
What am I doing?
They say my talent is worth pursuing,
But my talent only comes from the trauma that I've faced,
So keep me in your prayers because I don't know if it's too late,
I find it hard to talk to people so my poetry is the only way,
That's all I had to say.
You don't have to convince me that I'll be okay,
Because only time will tell whether or not I'll be saved.

Blay .G.

I became scared of the idea of living and accustomed to
the one of death,
I found comfort in the thoughts of not being around
anybody else,
I found pleasure in thrills of pushing myself to the edge,
Where I'm potentially putting my life at risk,
I keep telling myself I cannot be living like this
So I shouldn't do it again
Until the next time it happens.
I'm so used to this pattern,
It's only a matter of time,
Till I push it too far and my heartbeat flat lines.

I was. I am. I will be.

They say sleep is the cousin of death,
So I know that every time I blink I'm one step closer to
my last breath,
And every time I lay my head down to rest,
The cousins play and decide who will keep me next.
Eenie, Meenie, Minie Mo,
Does he stay or does he go?
Will he wake to live another day?
or will cousin death take him away?

Blay .G.

.

Have you ever felt what it's like contemplating your life,
With a knife on your right and your pen ready to write,
Why you're ready to see the light because you have no more energy in you to fight,
Just the thoughts of a happy ending by the end of the night,
The notes are written and addressed to whoever may find it,
Now you pick up the knife and decide whether it'll be the left or the right wrist,
Thoughts rushing through your head causing the tears to cover your iris,
Hoping and praying that it works the first time, give me the luck of the Irish,
Now the blades slit through the skin and the blood starts to show,
Your vision starts to blur,
Your heart is still beating but you can feel that it's getting slow,
this is all thoughts of a depressed sixteen-year-old.

I was. I am. I will be.

My poetry became somewhat of entertainment to them,
Something they could read in their spare time and share with their friends,
But did they know the tears that I shed when I think over these words?
Ink mixed with my tears, no wonder they see the pain in my verse,
I've wanted to let go so many times but I question whether it's the right decision to make,
The last thing I want to do is cause my loved ones any heartbreak,
But my head hurts, my hearts cold, my souls gone, I feel like I'm under constant attack,
Lord, you blessed me with a chance to experience earth but I'm done here now,
so please take me back.

Blay .G.

I often question what the outcome would be if life became too much and I decided it was my time to leave,
Would my enemies come to my funeral and lay down a couple of fake cries for me?
Put on a face and tell the crowd how together we share so many memories,
Would the girls from my past even be assed to attend?
Would they come by themselves or would they show up with their men?
How many of my so-called friends would feel the need to pretend?
To act like they're devastated when they're relieved they'll never have to see my face again,
Would my siblings regret any of the fights that we had?
Will I finally get the attention that I craved so much from my dad?
So many questions but no answers, but I'm in need to know,
I've now reached the point where I'm in need to go.
Sorry.

I was. I am. I will be.

My poetry has always been a mirror to the emotions that
I found it hard to express,
So, if this book suddenly comes to an end.
-

Just know I was too close to the edge.

Blay .G.

Honestly, I wish I could express to you every single
atom of pain I feel when I wake up but I've come to a
point where I don't even feel it anymore,
I know it's not normal to be immune to pain but my
happiness is like the rare shooting star,
There's excitement when it comes but it doesn't last for
long.
I try to talk to people but they'd rather talk about
themselves,
It can't be that bad if I leave because I'm already living
in hell,
It's like I have to wear a mask when I go out that
disguises these emotions,
Everyone says they got me but I've never seen so many
people lie with such devotion,
I'm here to help but there's no one to help me,
And the last breath I take may just allow me to set free,
These voices telling me to cut until my left wrist bleeds,
And since you love my poetry let me tell you a story:

Did you ever hear the one about the boy who constantly
wrote poetry about himself?
And every poem he wrote was a cry for help,
But all ever got was compliments and wows,
Because they didn't pay attention to the pain he was
going through until his body was found.

I was. I am. I will be.

My Face, thoughts, and feelings never equally correlate,
I could be feeling anxious but act confident for the sake of others,
Whilst my mind suffers, yet there's a smile of comfortability whilst it continues to wonder,
Questioning whether they like me or are they just being kind and accepting me,
But when I leave they talk about all the things that I wish I was and how I'm meant to be.
A social freak in the eyes of others I'm so misunderstood,
My soul is pure, it's good and if I could express it then I would,
But instead I'm just that awkward friend and this is why I'd much rather keep myself at home,
It may not be the most fun thing to do but at least I'm not judged when I'm on my own.

Blay .G.

Depression is a creeper it won't hit you like a ton of bricks,
You'll just think it's another bad day, so there's no need to pay attention to it,
But it continues and you notice that these bad days aren't changing,
When you socialise everyone's smiling so you feel compelled to do the same thing,
and still, this downwards feeling just doesn't seem to go away.
After a while, you get tired of putting on this face so you distance yourself from the people all around you,
Keep yourself in your room because you don't want to hear the noise outside like its soundproof and you don't want the sympathy you just want to be left alone.
A couple of texts on your phone along with many missed calls,
you try distractions but the things you loved the most have now turned into chores...

I was. I am. I will be.

I find it so hard to remain positive,
Especially when things keep happening that doesn't make sense,
But I understand that life is a suspense movie where God is the director,
So like every movie of this genre,
I guess it'll make sense in the end.
At least I hope so...

Blay .G.

Depression seems to be something I can't run away from because every time that I believe that it's gone, Here comes a surprise.
Suicide may be the first thing that I think about now because I'm alive,
But the truth is it won't make any difference because in my mind I've already died,
My eyes are already dried due to the constant tears that I've cried,
And as a man, I'm supposed to make sure my emotions are something that I hide,
but the truth is I've already tried with the broken smiles and constant lies,
I try to be the support for those who're going through it but now I've given up,
I'm sorry to you all, but it's my time, enough is enough.

I was. I am. I will be.

I don't write poetry.
They write themselves,
My mind is simply the womb,
And the pen is the vessel that helps give it life to the world.

Blay .G.

4

I was. I am. I will be.

Treat God as a Best friend,
Someone you can open up to without feeling judged,
Someone you can tell the good as well as the bad.
We tend to cry to him for help,
but ignore him in our bliss,
Tell me would you call someone your Best friend,
If they treated you like this?

Blay .G.

You see him as a mystical figure. A genie that you can call on at any time you are in need of him to grant your wishes. You see him as the backup plan, the person you call on when your life starts to spiral out of hand. I see him as my best friend, someone that's there for me throughout the good times and the bad. The person that celebrates with me throughout my highs but also the one who gives me a shoulder to cry on when I'm down. I see him as the friendly neighbour that I never fail to greet in the mornings whether there's sun or there's snow. I see him as the father figure who raised me to be the man that lives to perfect his heart of gold. I see him as the person I gave my heart to, a connection so intimate we both will never let go. I see him as the older sibling that I can talk to for advice knowing that they have my best interest at heart. You may doubt him when you're going through rough times and feel like you're alone but look back to the state you were in then compared to how far you've come now. I'm sure you'll realise that every one of those situations resulted in your growth.

I was. I am. I will be.

Think of a relationship like a table you're trying to put together from scratch,
Love is the surface, but without the screws which is the loyalty,
Without the legs which is the trust,
How do you expect the relationship to stand strong?
It takes more than just love.

Blay .G.

Trust is such a hard thing to give nowadays because no matter how clean hearted some people come across to be, they may very well be the ones that soil your opinion on the opposite gender. What you have to remember is that we live in a world of people that will uplift us and others that will break us. If you allow yourself to miss out on a good opportunity with someone that could bring value to your life because of what someone in the past took away from it, you're blocking your blessings.

It's fair to have your guard up and it's fair to take a break but do not allow yourself to give up completely knowing deep down there's someone out there for you.

I was. I am. I will be.

Some people will judge the book by its cover,
Others will judge by the chapter they happened to
stumble upon,
But the ones worth keeping around are those who'll
read the whole book,
yet still won't judge.

Blay .G.

Learning to love yourself is like learning how to drive a car.
Once you know, then you can invite a passenger to accompany you to your destination.
However,
if you don't know how to drive this car,
You risk terribly hurting yourself as well as the passenger you chose.

I was. I am. I will be.

Heartbreak is not the end of a movie,
But the beginning of a new scene.
Being unemployed does not necessarily mean you're stagnant,
It's preparation for miracles about to happen,
Failure is nothing more than a trip to the ground,
Are you prepared to stand back on your two feet?
Negativity will only keep you down,
If you accept defeat.

Blay .G.

If you love him then that pride can be pushed aside because some people only get one chance to meet the love of their life,
So how're you allowing yourself to lose a blessing because at that moment you feel he's not acting right?
How're you allowing yourself to lose a gift that God went out of his way to provide?
Knowing that God may not give you the same opportunity twice,
Don't get me wrong if its long and your energy is getting drained,
Then, by all means, don't let that man drive you insane,
But if he's real and he's genuine but you're going through a rough patch,
Don't give up on something that'll be difficult to get back.

I was. I am. I will be.

You had seeds of doubt that flourished into crops of
certainty,
You refused to believe that he broke his loyalty,
Why would he hurt you purposely?
"Maybe I wasn't good enough".
NO, it's him that wasn't worthy,
But don't worry those tears can only help wash away the
pain from your mind,
From your heart, From your soul,
and help plant a new crop,
where he left an empty
hole.

Blay .G.

The hardest thing to be in is a toxic relationship with someone you are still in love with. We often learn to tolerate the hurt to experience potential happiness. A happiness that you once had in hope that it may come back because if it's happened once then it can happen again right? Wrong. Sometimes people outgrow each other or grow apart and no matter how much you don't want to accept the painful reality, you need to do what's best for both of you. At the time it may not feel good, but neither does the rainstorm before the shine. When you're ill, the remedies to get better are not usually appealing but the results are always worth it. You know what you need to do but usually, the hardest part is actually doing it. If you are currently in this situation be wise. The temporary sadness will be worth the long term feeling of relief.

I was. I am. I will be.

You may believe in having a soulmate but I believe in soulmates. This world has a population of 7 billion people. Every day the actions we make dictate what happens next in our lives and where we end up. One decision can change us from going down one road to another. This will then lead us to meet new people that we would have potentially never met if we'd chosen to go down the other road. I believe that there are many people that are on this earth that could be classed as our soulmates but we'll never meet them simply for the fact of not choosing to pursue a certain journey in life. If you break up with one person or somehow lose this person, no they can never be replaced, that is true. However, this does not mean you will never feel what it is to be loved or fall in love again. In such a populated planet that we live on, there will always be someone else out there for you. It's all about having the patience and waiting until you finally cross paths.

Blay .G.

We are simply mountains of different heights searching for the person that's willing to risk the hike,
Don't cry over the people that gave up halfway because they decided that the top was too high to reach,
But be thankful that they made space for the ones that took their time and efforts to climb and finally reach your mountain peak.

I was. I am. I will be.

Sometimes a conversation with yourself is needed. We get so caught up with the busyness of everyday life that we don't make time for ourselves to recognise some issues we may be facing. At times when something has gone wrong, we'd rather turn a blind eye to it and continue with life but turning away from these issues don't make them disappear. What is it in you that makes you so angry when someone talks to you a certain way? Why is it that you cannot trust people? What is stopping you from being happy? Don't ignore the answers to these questions. Once you have found the answer then try to find a solution. A problem ignored is only a problem suppressed. One thing about the brain is that anything suppressed will come out one day and if left too long it will be in its most rotten form. Don't allow yourself to become a bitter individual when you have the ability to become a better individual.

Blay .G.

It was through being told that I'm not enough that I learned my worth.
It was by being rejected by the ones I love that I learned to put myself first.
It was through the tears and the trauma that I saw the light.
It was through the evil of the day, that I learned to appreciate the beauty of the night.

I was. I am. I will be.

Being carefree does not necessarily mean taking pictures with flowers in your hair and being wild. The art of being carefree is simply accepting yourself, loving yourself and not being afraid to show who you truly are.

Blay .G.

God's timing does not consist of hands on the clock,
It consists of his hands removing life's obstacles when
you physically can not. He is all you will have in the end
so put your trust in him
When you're freed by his grace, you cannot be blocked
by anything.

I was. I am. I will be.

They say there's plenty fish in the sea,
But there's not another like you,
You found it in your heart to love me,
I pray that another might too.

"How did you know that you were in love?"

"When I couldn't remember having a life before I met her"

"But how did you know that it had come to an end?"

"When my thoughts of happiness came from our history rather than from the person that was with me."

I was. I am. I will be.

Throughout my life, I have learned that perception is a deception,
We often focus on the bad and forget to look in the right direction,
Try to focus on the good things so you can attract more
Your mindset will be the reason that you rise or you fall.

Blay .G.

To the women of my past, I was simply a caterpillar. To the woman of my future, I will be the butterfly. Right now I am in the cocoon learning, growing and molding myself into the person that I pray you desire. I tried many times to turn the page to become a better person but I realised I was still living within the same genre. It was time I closed the book I was living and write one of my own. One in which you will appear within the first chapter and stay until the glossary. I'm so misunderstood, It's as if I'm a foreigner surrounded by locals of the land but not even you would need Rosetta stone to understand that I'll always put your heart before mine no matter how damaged I am. I believed I was the best at my craft until I saw a peek of what God has written in the stars for us, true poetry. I still haven't mastered the art of love, but I'm an apprentice in training. I'm still learning what it takes to love and be loved. If I'm ever tested, I hope that I'll be rewarded with your heart when I pass.

I was. I am. I will be.

I didn't come from much,
And not to say I had it tough or was poor,
But the children around me always seemed to have more,
I remember nights sleeping on the wooden floor, with a portable heater because the electricity didn't work,
And waking up with cramps in my neck but when I was asked what was wrong I had to pretend it didn't hurt,
Because I didn't want my dad to feel any worse.
No duvet, no comfort of a pillow, just my dad and myself in a mini studio,
Where we slept was where we ate and kept ourselves entertained,
Same place I learned to write when I kept my self-locked away,
Dreaming for better days, and I guess that they came, but by then it was too late.
They say you're a product of your environment, well look what mine made,
I cried and cried and till my tear ducts dried up and my soul went missing, now I can't find her, and I find it harder to be emotional without writing because I learned that this is the only way that I can express my pain and if you want to get know me further I guess that can be booked, but you won't hear it face to face, so you just have to wait for the next book.

Printed in Great Britain
by Amazon